Music Minus One Trumpet

12231

Come Fly With Me

Glenn Zottola

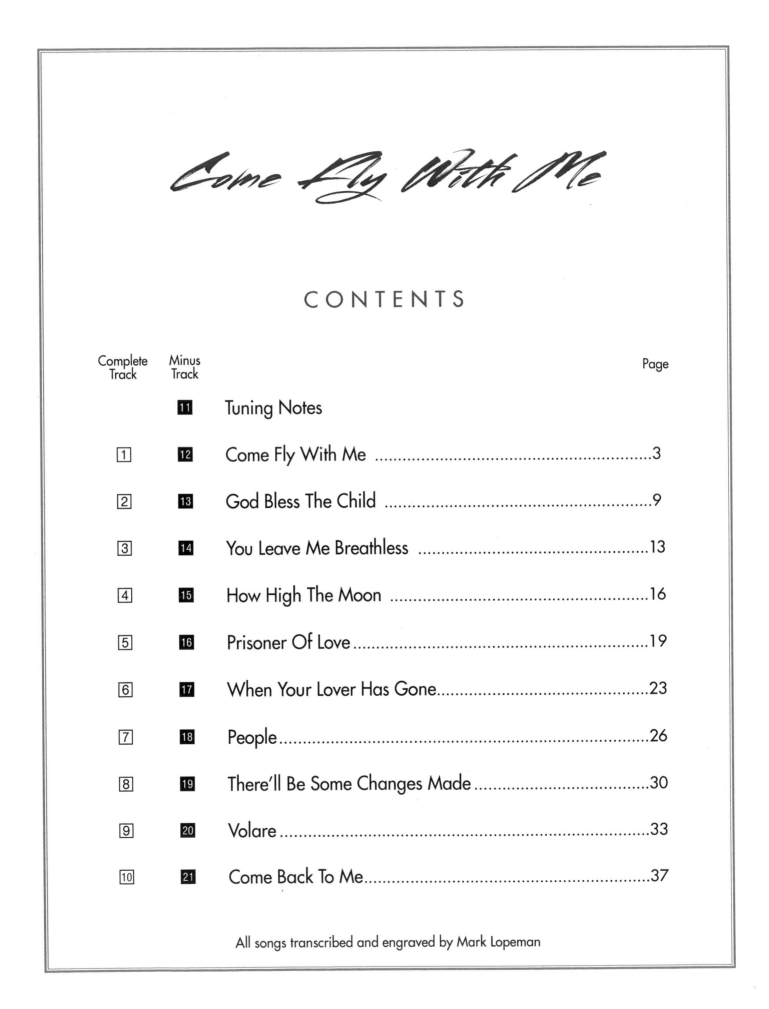

Come Fly With Me

CONTENTS

All songs transcribed and engraved by Mark Lopeman

ISBN 978-1-941566-94-7

SOLO Bb TRUMPET

Come Fly With Me

music by
Jimmy Van Heusen
lyrics by
Sammy Cahn

MMO 12231

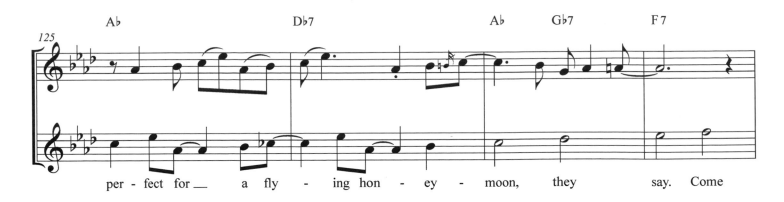

per - fect for ___ a fly - ing hon - ey - moon, they say. Come

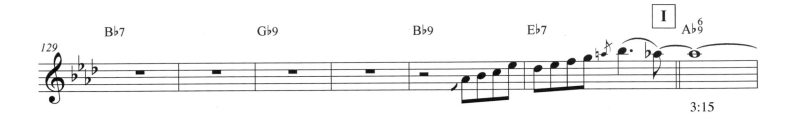

3:15

SOLO Bb TRUMPET

God Bless The Child

from BUBBLING
BROWN SUGAR
music and lyrics by
Billie Holiday
and
Arthur Herzog, Jr.

GLENN'S SOLO

ORIG. MELODY

0:27

Them that's got shall get, them that's

not shall lose, so the Bib - le says, and it still is news.

Ma - ma may have, Pa - pa may have, but God bless the child that's

MMO 12231

12

SOLO Bb TRUMPET

You Leave Me Breathless

from the Paramount motion picture
COCONUT GROVE
music by
Friedrich Hollander
words by
Ralph Freed

more, be-cause,_____ you take my breath a - way._____

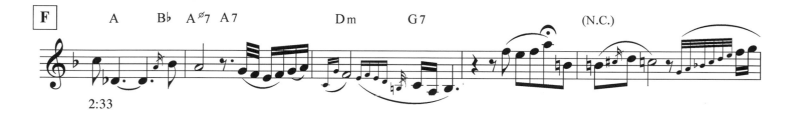

2:33

SOLO Bb TRUMPET

How High The Moon

from TWO FOR THE SHOW
music by
Morgan Lewis
lyrics by
Nancy Hamilton

me as I love you. Some - where there's mu - sic,_____ it's where you

are._____ Some - where there's heav - en,_____ how near, how

far!_____ The dark - est night would shine if you would come to me soon._____

___ Un - til you will, how still my heart, how high the moon!_____

SOLO Bb TRUMPET

Prisoner Of Love

words and music by
Leo Robin, Russ Columbo
and Clarence Gaskill

A-lone from night to night you'll find me, too weak to break the chains that bind me; I need no shack-les to re-mind me, I'm just a pris-'ner of love.

For one com-mand I stand and wait now, from one who's mas-ter of my

MMO 12231

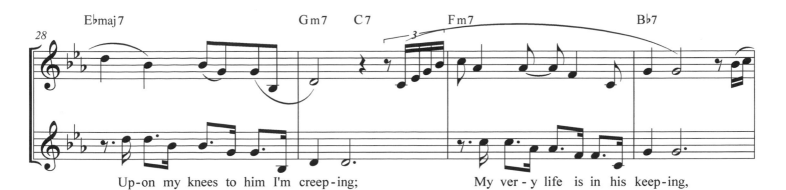

Up-on my knees to him I'm creep-ing; My ver-y life is in his keep-ing,

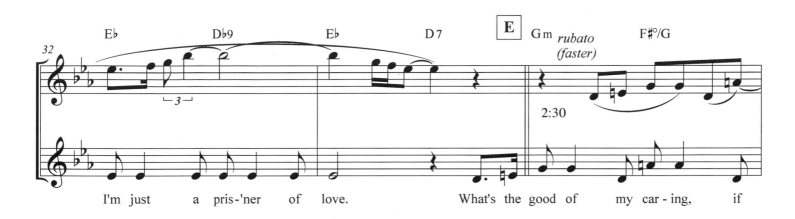

I'm just a pris-'ner of love. What's the good of my car-ing, if

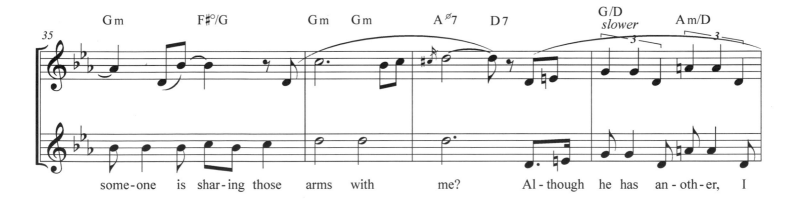

some-one is shar-ing those arms with me? Al-though he has an-oth-er, I

can't have an-oth-er, for I'm not free. He's in my dreams, a-wake or

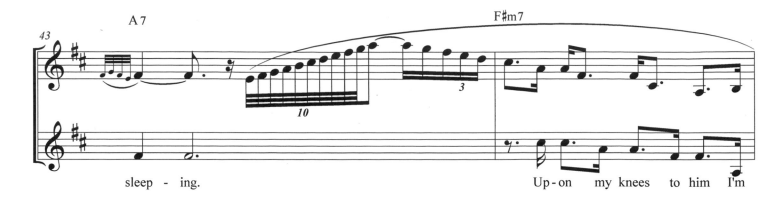

sleep - ing.

Up - on my knees to him I'm

creep -   ing;

My ver - y life is in his keep - ing,

SOLO Bb TRUMPET

When Your Lover Has Gone

words and music by
Einar Aaron Swan

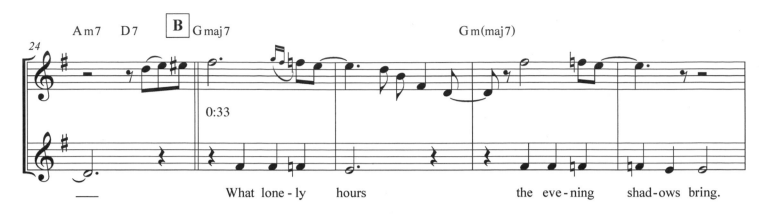

What lone - ly hours   the eve - ning shad - ows bring.

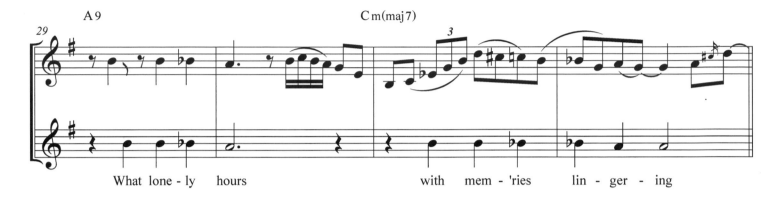

What lone - ly hours   with mem - 'ries lin - ger - ing

like fad - ed flow'rs;   life can't mean an - y - thing   when your

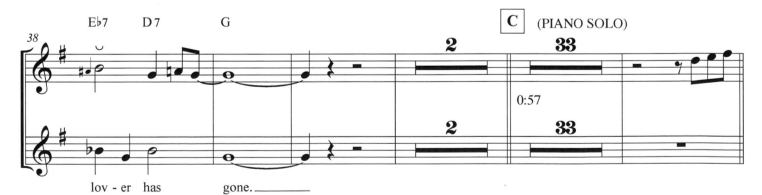

lov - er has gone. _____

SOLO Bb TRUMPET

People

from FUNNY GIRL
music by
Jule Styne
lyrics by
Bob Merrill

MMO 12231

G

peo - ple _____ peo-ple who need peo - ple _____ are the luck-i-est peo-ple

in the world! _____

SOLO Bb TRUMPET

There'll Be Some Changes Made

music by
Benton Overstreet
lyrics by
William Blackstone

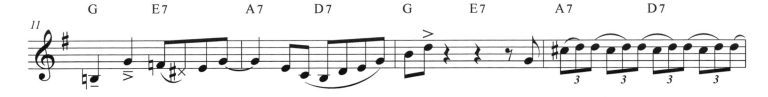

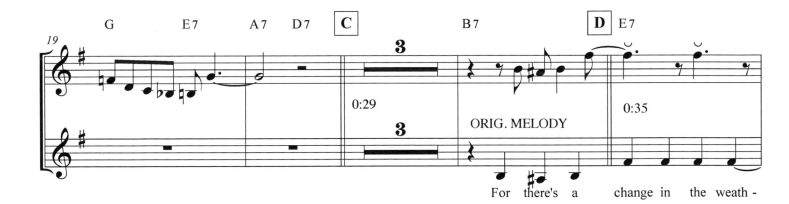

MMO 12231

there'll be some chan - ges made.

(SAX SOLO)

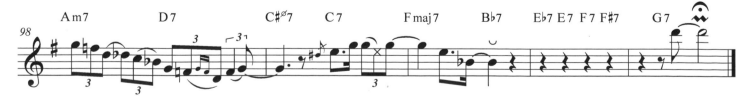

SOLO Bb TRUMPET

Volare

music and original lyrics by
Franco Migliacci and
Dominico Modugno
English lyrics by
Mitchell Parish

MMO 12231

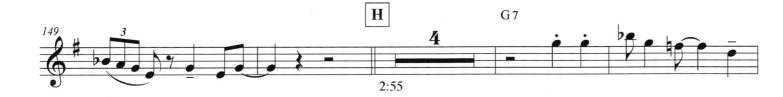

from ON A CLEAR
DAY YOU CAN SEE
FOREVER
music by
Burton Lane
lyrics by
Alan J. Lerner

SOLO Bb TRUMPET

Come Back To Me

Music Minus One
50 Executive Boulevard • Elmsford, New York 10523-1325
914-592-1188 • e-mail: info@musicminusone.com
www.musicminusone.com

MMO 12231

ISBN 978-1-941566-94-7